BENJAMIN WHITE

POETRY UNLOCKED

A Student's Guide to
Interpreting Poetic Expression

POETRY UNLOCKED

A Student's Guide to
Interpreting Poetic Expression

BENJAMIN WHITE

AI disclaimer:

To illustrate some core concepts, I have used generative AI to create digestible examples. This serves as an illustration of the technique, not as a replacement for the work of a poet. Poetry, by its very essence, is the unveiling of the human experience – an aspect that AI cannot, and will never be able to, replace.

Published in 2025 by Amba Press, Melbourne, Australia
www.ambapress.com.au

© Benjamin White 2025

All rights reserved. No part of this book may be reproduced or transmitted in any form or by any means, electronic or mechanical, including photocopying, recording or by any information storage and retrieval system, without prior permission in writing from the publisher.

Cover design: Tess McCabe
Internal design: Midlands
Editor: Rica Dearman

ISBN: 9781923215849 (pbk)
ISBN: 9781923215856 (ebk)

A catalogue record for this book is available from the National Library of Australia.

Contents

Introduction		1
Chapter 1	What makes a poem?	3
Chapter 2	The tools of poetry	11
Chapter 3	Exploring poetic forms	19
Chapter 4	The heart of poetry: Exploring themes	29
Chapter 5	The art of word choice	37
Chapter 6	Analysing poetry	45
Chapter 7	Writing about poetry	53
Chapter 8	Poetry through time and culture	61
Chapter 9	Poetry in the digital age	71
Chapter 10	Your poetry portfolio	81
Key terms		87

Introduction

Hey there! Welcome to this book about poetry. I've written it, just like all my other books, with you, the student, in mind. My goal with this book is to make poetry less intimidating and more accessible. We all have to study poetry at some point in our schooling, and let's be honest, it's not always the most exciting subject – I'm including teachers in that statement, too!

Poetry Unlocked is designed to break down the building blocks of poetry – devices, forms, themes – and guide you through creating your own portfolio of work. It comprises both analytical and creative responses, so you can explore both sides of the coin.

I've included a diverse range of poems and poets from Australia and around the world. Some you might be familiar with, while others might be new to you. That's perfectly fine! We're all here to learn and grow.

I hope this book helps you on your poetry journey. Happy reading!

CHAPTER 1

What makes a poem?

What makes a poem different from a story, song or even a meme? Is it the way it looks, sounds or feels? Poems have been written for thousands of years, yet their power hasn't faded. Poetry can connect us to others, give us a voice and make the ordinary extraordinary.

In this chapter, we'll explore the building blocks of poetry. You'll learn what makes poetry unique, read examples that showcase its qualities and begin thinking like a poet. By the end of the chapter, you'll not only understand the key elements of poetry, but you'll also take your first steps toward creating your own.

> **Before we begin**
>
> What comes to mind when you hear the word 'poetry'? Write down three words or phrases. Don't overthink it – just jot down your first thoughts.

Key elements of poetry

Poetry stands out because of its unique use of language, structure and sound. Here are the key elements that make a poem a poem:

1. **Concentrated language:** Poets often say more with fewer words. Each word carries weight and is chosen carefully for its meaning, sound and emotional impact.

2. **Structure:** Poems have their own architecture. Line breaks, stanzas and white space guide how we read and feel a poem. The way a poem is laid out on the page can emphasise certain ideas or emotions.

3. **Sound:** Poetry is music made from words. Poets use rhythm, rhyme and sound devices to create a memorable experience. Some of the ways poets make their poems 'sing' are:

    - Alliteration: Repeated sounds at the start of words (for example, 'silver snakes slithered')

    - Assonance: Repeated vowel sounds (for example, 'the cool moon')

    - Rhythm: The beat of the poem, created by syllable patterns

4. **Multiple meanings:** Poems often invite interpretation. A single line can carry many layers of meaning, depending on the reader's perspective.

Case study: William Carlos Williams' 'This Is Just to Say'

This short poem looks like a note left on the fridge, but it's a perfect example of poetry's magic:

I have eaten
the plums
that were in
the ice box

and which
you were probably
saving
for breakfast

Forgive me
they were delicious
so sweet
and so cold

Analysis

1. Concentrated language:
   - The poem is only 29 words, yet it creates a vivid image and evokes emotions.
   - 'So sweet' and 'so cold' captures the sensory experience of eating the plums.

2. Structure:
   - The short lines and irregular breaks mimic the casual tone of a note but force the reader to pause and reflect.

3. Sound:
   - The repetition of 's' sounds (sweet, saving, so) adds softness and flow.

Discussion questions

1. How does the structure impact how you read the poem?
2. Is the speaker truly sorry – or are they enjoying their confession?

Poetry in practice – poetry in everyday life

Objective

Recognise poetry in the ordinary.

Your task

1. Look around your home, school or neighbourhood. Find an object or moment that seems unremarkable (for example, a lunchbox, a rainy window or a pair of sneakers).

2. Write a short paragraph describing this object. Focus on:

    - How it looks: colours, shapes, textures
    - How it feels: emotions or memories it triggers

3. Rewrite your description as a poem. Use line breaks and vivid language to transform the ordinary into something extraordinary.

How poems work

Think of a poem like a recipe. It combines ingredients (words, images, sounds) with techniques to create something unique. Here are three tools poets use:

Tool	What it does	Example
Imagery	Creates pictures in the reader's mind	*The golden sun spilled into the sea*
Alliteration	Repeats sounds to create rhythm	*Silver snakes slithered softly*
Line breaks	Shapes how we read and pause	*The cat / waits / by the door*

Building confidence

Reading poetry can feel challenging, especially when encountering complex language or unfamiliar structures. That's why starting with simpler texts and gradually moving to more complex ones can make a big difference.

By beginning with easier examples, like nursery rhymes or short free verse poems, you can build confidence in understanding rhythm, imagery and meaning. As you progress, you'll develop the tools to tackle classic and modern poetry with ease.

1. **Begin with a nursery rhyme** (like 'Twinkle, Twinkle, Little Star')
   - Consider its rhythm, rhyme and imagery.
   - Highlight how simple words create a visual and emotional connection.

2. **Progress to a short free verse poem** (like 'The Red Wheelbarrow' by William Carlos Williams)
   - Consider how meaning is created through line breaks and imagery despite the lack of rhyme or rhythm.
3. **Analyse a classic poem excerpt** (like a stanza from 'I Wandered Lonely as a Cloud' by William Wordsworth)
   - If you're feeling bold, dig into the metaphor, tone and sound patterns.

Final thought

Poetry isn't about rules – it's about noticing, imagining and connecting. As you move through this book, you'll learn to read, analyse and create poems that reflect your unique voice.

> ### Reflection
> Revisit the three words you wrote at the start of this chapter about poetry. What new words would you add to your list?

Activity: The anatomy of a poem

Learning intention

To consolidate your understanding of poetic elements by analysing a poem and reflecting on how its structure, language and sound create meaning.

Your task

Step 1: Select a poem

Choose a short poem (from this chapter or another provided by your teacher). Examples include William Carlos Williams' 'This Is Just to Say' or a poem of your choice.

Step 2: Annotate the poem

Highlight the following elements:

- **Language** – words or phrases that stand out for their vividness or precision
- **Structure** – line breaks, stanzas or white space
- **Sound** – repetition, rhythm or musicality

Step 3: Reflect

Write a short paragraph explaining how these elements work together to create meaning or emotion in the poem.

Step 4: Portfolio connection

Save your annotated poem and your reflection.

In Chapter 10, you will refine this analysis for inclusion in your final portfolio.

CHAPTER 2

The tools of poetry

Poetry isn't just about words – it's about what poets do with them. Poets use a range of tools to make their work vivid, musical and meaningful. In the English classroom we like to call these 'poetic devices'. These devices include imagery, sound devices, rhythm and figurative language. Just like a painter uses brushes and colours, poets use language to create pictures, evoke emotions and connect with their audience.

In this chapter, we'll explore these devices in detail. You'll learn how they work, why they matter and how you can use them in your own writing. By the end of the chapter, you'll have experimented with some of these techniques and built confidence with your own poetic voice.

> **Before we begin**
>
> What devices do poets use to create their art? Write down three things that you think make a poem powerful or memorable.

Poetic devices and how they work

1. Imagery: Painting pictures with words

Imagery appeals to the senses, helping the audience to see, hear, feel or even taste what the poet describes.

What it does: Makes poetry vivid and relatable.

Example: *The golden sun spilled fire into the sea.*

Annotation: The audience can visualise the sun setting over the ocean.

Quick practice: Describe an everyday object (for example, your phone, a tree outside) using sensory details. Focus on sight, sound or touch.

2. Sound devices: Making words sing

Sound devices give poetry its musical quality.

Types of sound devices:

Alliteration: Repeating the same consonant sound.

Example: *Silver snakes slithered softly.*

Assonance: Repeating vowel sounds.

Example: *The cool moon rose soon.*

Onomatopoeia: Words that imitate sounds.

Example: *The leaves crackled underfoot.*

Quick practice: Write one sentence using alliteration and assonance.

3. Rhythm: The beat of a poem

Rhythm is created by the pattern of stressed and unstressed syllables.

What it does: Guides how a poem flows and feels.

Example: *I wandered lonely as a cloud.*

Annotation: The steady rhythm creates a calm, reflective mood.

Quick practice: Choose a favourite song lyric or a line of poetry. Clap along to its rhythm to identify the stressed and unstressed syllables.

4. Rhyme: Connecting sounds

Rhyme is the repetition of similar sounds, usually at the end of lines in a poem. Poets use rhyme to create rhythm, connection and emphasis.

Types of rhyme:

Perfect rhyme: Words sound identical (for example, 'sky' and 'fly').

Slant rhyme: Words sound similar but not identical (for example, 'move' and 'love').

Internal rhyme: Rhymes occur within the same line (for example, I 'see', the 'tree', so 'free').

Quick practice: Write a short four-line poem that uses at least one type of rhyme. Experiment with perfect, slant or internal rhyme.

5. Figurative language: Going beyond the literal

Poets use figurative language to add depth and layers of meaning to their work.

Types of figurative language:

Metaphor: Comparing two things *without* using 'like' or 'as'.

Example: *Her smile was the sunrise.*

Simile: Comparing two things using 'like' or 'as'.

Example: *Her smile was like the sunrise.*

Personification: Giving human qualities to non-human things.

Example: *The wind whispered through the trees.*

Quick practice: Write one metaphor or simile about something you see right now.

Poetry in practice – poetic device box

Use the devices from this chapter to create a short poem inspired by an everyday object or moment.

Choose your subject

It could be your favourite snack, the sound of rain or a messy desk.

Apply the devices

- Use imagery to describe it.
- Add sound devices to enhance its musicality.
- Experiment with figurative language to give it deeper meaning.

Example

Subject: A pencil

Imagery: *The wooden body splinters under pressure.*

Sound: *Scratch, scribble, scrape.*

Figurative language: *It's a sword that turns thoughts into stories, carving up the page.*

Note: Save your poem draft for your final portfolio. You'll revise and refine it in later chapters.

Case study: Langston Hughes' 'Dreams'

Langston Hughes' poem 'Dreams' is short but powerful, showing how poetic tools can create a deep meaning.

Hold fast to dreams
For if dreams die
Life is a broken-winged bird
That cannot fly.

Hold fast to dreams
For when dreams go
Life is a barren field
Frozen with snow.

Annotations

1. Imagery – *broken-winged bird* and *barren field frozen with snow* create vivid mental pictures.
2. Metaphor – dreams are compared to essential parts of life, like birds and fertile fields.
3. Repetition – the phrase *Hold fast to dreams* emphasises its central message.

Discussion questions

1. How does the poet use imagery to make the reader care about dreams?
2. Why do you think Hughes repeats the phrase *Hold fast to dreams*?

Poetry is everywhere

Poetry isn't just for classrooms or books – it's all around you. From song lyrics to sports commentary, poetry shows up in unexpected places. It adds beauty, rhythm and meaning to our everyday lives – maybe in ways you haven't thought of before. Take a look.

In song lyrics and rap

Listen to Eminem's 'Lose Yourself': *His palms are sweaty, knees weak, arms are heavy*. The rhythm and internal rhyme make these words stick in your head.

Or, for the Swifties out there, consider Tay Tay's 'All Too Well': *Autumn leaves falling down like pieces into place* – a simile that perfectly captures both a visual image and a feeling.

In advertising

Advertisers know the power of poetic devices:

- *Red Bull gives you wings*. (Metaphor)
- *Maybe she's born with it, maybe it's Maybelline*. (Repetition)
- *Don't dream it. Drive it*. (Alliteration)
- *Snap! Crackle! Pop!* (Onomatopoeia)

In sports commentary

Listen to any sports broadcast:

- *He's a freight train heading for the goal posts!*
- *The ball dances through the defence!*
- *Lightning speed from the young striker.*

These aren't just descriptions – they're metaphors and personification; devices that bring the game to life.

Final thought

Poetic devices are like keys – they unlock new ways of seeing the world and expressing how it makes us feel and think. As you move through this book, keep experimenting with these devices to discover your unique voice as a poet.

Reflection

Revisit the three things you wrote at the beginning of this chapter about the devices poets use. Did anything surprise you? What new devices would you add to your list?

Activity: Poetic devices in action

Learning intention

To consolidate your understanding of poetic devices by experimenting with their use in your own writing and preparing for the final portfolio task.

Your task

Step 1: Choose a theme

Select a theme or subject that interests you, such as nature, relationships or a personal experience.

Step 2: Use three poetic devices

Write a four- to six-line poem using **three poetic devices** you've learned in this chapter.

Choose from:

- Imagery
- Alliteration
- Assonance
- Rhythm
- Metaphor
- Simile
- Personification

Step 3: Experiment with language

Focus on making your language vivid and expressive. Think about how your chosen devices enhance the mood, meaning or sound of your poem.

Step 4: Portfolio connection

Save your poem for your portfolio. This draft will demonstrate your ability to apply poetic devices in creative writing. In later chapters, you can refine it further.

CHAPTER 3

Exploring poetic forms

The shape of a poem is just as important as its words. Poets use structure – like line breaks, stanzas and specific forms – to control how a poem looks, sounds and feels. Some poems follow strict rules, like a haiku or a sonnet, while others, like free verse, flow without limitations.

In this chapter, we'll explore different poetic forms. From traditional to modern, you'll learn how these forms shape meaning and emotion, and experiment with writing your own. By the end of the chapter, you'll have created two poems in different forms to include in your portfolio.

> ### Before we begin
> Take a moment to think about how poems are structured. What comes to mind when you think of a poem's shape or structure? Write down three words or ideas.

What are poetic forms?

A poetic form is the structure or set of rules a poem follows. Let's look at some of the most common forms (I bet you've heard of at least one of these):

1. Haiku: The power of simplicity

Structure: Three lines, 5-7-5 syllable pattern.

What it does: Captures a single moment or feeling, often inspired by nature.

2. Sonnet: Beauty in rhyme and rhythm

Structure: Fourteen lines, typically written in iambic pentameter (10 syllables per line).

What it does: Explores complex themes like love, time or identity.

3. Free verse: Breaking the rules

Structure: No set rules for rhyme or rhythm.

What it does: Allows poets to write freely, focusing on the flow of ideas.

4. Acrostic: Hidden messages

Structure: The first letter of each line spells out a word or phrase.

What it does: Adds a playful or secretive element to the poem.

5. Concrete poetry: Art on the page

Structure: The poem's shape or layout on the page reflects its meaning.

What it does: Combines visual art with language to create an image.

6. Slam poetry: Performance and passion

Structure: No strict rules – slam poetry is meant to be performed.

What it does: Combines rhythm, emotion and storytelling to connect with a live audience.

7. Ballad/bush ballad: Telling a story

Structure: A narrative poem with quatrains (four-line stanzas) and a rhyme scheme (for example, ABAB). Often set to music.

What it does: Tells a story, often with a sense of rhythm and repetition.

8. Limerick: Light and playful

Structure: Five lines with an AABBA rhyme scheme. The first, second and fifth lines are longer, while the third and fourth are shorter.

What it does: Creates humour or light-heartedness.

9. Blackout poetry: Words in the shadows

Structure: Created by blacking out words on a page of text, leaving selected words visible to form a poem.

What it does: Focuses on simplicity, creativity and discovering unexpected meanings.

Understanding rhyme schemes

Rhyme schemes are the patterns of rhyming words at the end of lines in a poem. They're written using letters to represent the sounds at the end of each line. For example:

1. Simple rhyme scheme: ABAB

   > Roses are red (A)
   > Violets are blue (B)
   > Sugar is sweet (A)
   > And so are you (B)

2. Couplets: AA BB

   > The sun is bright, (A)
   > It warms the night, (A)
   > The stars will shine, (B)
   > Their light divine. (B)

3. Limerick: AABBA

   Limericks use a specific rhyme and rhythm pattern:

   > There once was a man from Peru, (A)
   > Who dreamed he was eating his shoe. (A)
   > He awoke with a fright (B)
   > In the middle of the night (B)
   > To find that his dream had come true. (A)

4. Sonnet: ABAB CDCD EFEF GG

   Sonnets often follow a more complex rhyme scheme. Here's the first quatrain of Shakespeare's 'Sonnet 18':

   > Shall I compare thee to a summer's day? (A)
   > Thou art more lovely and more temperate. (B)
   > Rough winds do shake the darling buds of May, (A)
   > And summer's lease hath all too short a date. (B)

What's behind the forms?

Poetic forms evolved for specific purposes across diverse cultures and times. Understanding where these forms came from helps us see why they work the way they do.

1. Sonnets originated during the 13th century in Italy and flourished in royal courts. Their 14-line structure perfectly suited complex emotional arguments – the first eight lines would present a problem or situation, while the final six lines offered a resolution or twist. This made them ideal for exploring matters of love, politics and internal conflict.

2. Haiku appeared from Japanese Buddhist traditions of mindfulness and presence. Their brief form forces the poet to focus on a single moment or image, much like meditation focuses the mind on the present. The traditional focus on seasons connects human experience to the natural world.

3. Slam poetry burst onto the scene in 1980s Chicago, giving voice to communities that felt excluded from traditional literary circles. Its emphasis on performance, rhythm and direct expression made poetry accessible and immediate, turning it from a written art into a powerful live experience.

4. Concrete poetry (also called shape or visual poetry) developed as poets realised that how words look on the page could be just as meaningful as how they sounded. By arranging words to create images, poets found they could make meaning work on multiple levels at once.

5. Epic poetry predates written language when stories had to be memorable enough to pass down orally. Features like regular rhythm, repetition and formulaic phrases helped people remember and retell these important cultural narratives.

Poetry in practice – try on a poetic form

Choose a form
- Haiku
- Sonnet
- Free verse
- Acrostic
- Concrete poetry
- Slam poetry

Write your poem
- Follow the rules of your chosen form.
- Focus on a specific theme or idea that inspires you (for example, nature, identity, a memory).

Reflect
- How did the form influence what you wrote?
- Did the structure help or challenge you?

Portfolio connection
- Save your poem for your portfolio. Later chapters will help you refine and expand it.

Finding the right form for you

Think of poetry forms like different containers; just as you wouldn't use a teacup to serve soup or a bowl to drink coffee, different poetic forms serve different purposes. Each form has its own strengths and creates different effects. Here are some forms and their themes or goals:

Theme/goal	Best form
Capture a single moment	Haiku or concrete poetry
Tell a story	Ballad or narrative free verse
Explore emotions	Sonnet or free verse
Create something playful	Limerick or acrostic
Experiment with structure	Free verse, blackout poetry

How form shapes meaning

The form of a poem isn't just about rules – it's about how those rules shape the meaning. A haiku's brevity forces us to focus on one image or idea, while a sonnet's rhythm creates a musical, reflective tone. Free verse, on the other hand, mirrors the unpredictability of thought or emotion.

Think of form as the container for a poet's ideas. Whether the container is rigid or fluid, it impacts how we experience the poem.

Case study: Contrasting forms

Compare two poems about the same theme but in different forms:

Concrete poetry

A poem about a tree might visually resemble a tree, with the words forming branches and leaves:

Reaching
Upward to the
Sun, branches spread
And whisper

Slam poetry

A performance piece about the same theme might use rhythm and emotion to emphasise a tree's strength:

It stands, rooted in time –
A witness to storms, to wars
To the laughter of children
Who climb its arms

Discussion questions

1. How does the structure of each poem shape its tone and impact?
2. Which form feels more effective to you? Why?
3. Could you rewrite one of these poems in another form (for example, a haiku)?

Final thought

The form of a poem is like its frame – it shapes how we see the picture inside. As you move forward, keep experimenting with forms to find the ones that best suit your voice and ideas.

> ### Reflection
>
> Revisit the three words or ideas you wrote at the beginning of this chapter about a poem's shape or structure. How has your understanding of poetic forms evolved?

Activity: Form challenge

Learning intention

To consolidate your understanding of poetic forms by writing two poems in contrasting forms for inclusion in your portfolio.

Your task

Step 1: Choose two forms

Pick two forms from this chapter (for example, haiku and slam poetry, or concrete and free verse).

Step 2: Write a poem in each form

Use the same theme for both poems (for example, memory, dream or nature).

Step 3: Reflect on the process

How did the forms shape your approach to the theme?

Which form felt more natural to you?

Step 4: Portfolio connection

Save both poems for your portfolio. These will demonstrate your ability to experiment with and adapt to different poetic structures.

CHAPTER 4

The heart of poetry: Exploring themes

What do poets write about? The answer is simple: everything. Poets explore the big questions – about love, life and death – but they also write about the small details of everyday life. From the beauty of nature to the complexity of human emotions, poetry allows us to express what's important to us in ways that are unique and meaningful.

In this chapter, we'll explore some of the most common themes in poetry. You'll read examples that bring these themes to life and reflect on how themes connect to your own experiences. By the end of the chapter, you'll begin brainstorming ideas for your own poetry portfolio, inspired by the themes that matter most to you.

> ### Before we begin
> What do you think poets write about most often? Write down three themes or topics that come to mind. At the end of the chapter, you'll revisit your list and see what has changed.

Common themes in poetry

Poets often revisit universal themes that resonate across time and cultures. Here are some of the most common:

1. Love

Love in poetry can be romantic, platonic or even self-love. It captures joy, heartbreak, longing and connection.

Example: From Elizabeth Barrett Browning's 'Sonnet 43':

> *How do I love thee? Let me count the ways.*
> *I love thee to the depth and breadth and height*
> *My soul can reach, when feeling out of sight*
> *For the ends of being and ideal grace.*

2. Nature

Nature is a constant source of inspiration for poets – especially the Romantics – who explore its beauty, power and connection to humanity.

Example: From William Wordsworth's 'I Wandered Lonely as a Cloud':

> *I wandered lonely as a cloud*
> *That floats on high o'er vales and hills,*
> *When all at once I saw a crowd,*
> *A host, of golden daffodils.*

3. Identity and self-discovery

Poetry allows us to reflect on who we are and how we see ourselves in the world.

Example: From Maya Angelou's 'Phenomenal Woman':

> *It's in the reach of my arms,*
> *The span of my hips,*
> *The stride of my step,*
> *The curl of my lips.*

4. Loss and grief

Poets often use their words to process and express emotions around loss, creating space for reflection and healing.

Example: From Dylan Thomas's 'Do Not Go Gentle into That Good Night':

> *Do not go gentle into that good night,*
> *Old age should burn and rave at close of day;*
> *Rage, rage against the dying of the light.*

5. Social and political issues

Poetry can be a tool for advocacy and activism, shining a light on injustice and inspiring change.

Example: From Oodgeroo Noonuccal's 'We Are Going':

> *The scrubs are gone,*
> *The hunting and the laughter.*
> *The eagle is gone,*
> *The emu and the kangaroo are gone from this place.*
> *The bora ring is gone.*
> *The corroboree is gone.*
> *And we are going.*

The heart of poetry: Exploring themes

Finding the theme

Themes are not always obvious. Poets use language, imagery and structure to suggest deeper meaning. Follow these steps to find the theme of a poem:

1. **Read the poem carefully**
   - Read the poem multiple times, both silently and aloud.
   - Pay attention to your first impressions – what feelings or ideas does the poem evoke?

2. **Look for clues**
   - Imagery – what pictures or scenes does the poet describe?
   - Word choice – what words stand out? Are they emotional, descriptive or symbolic?

3. **Ask questions**
   - Who is the speaker, and what are they experiencing or feeling?
   - What is the poem's tone (for example, joyful, sad, angry)?
   - What message or ideas does the poem seem to explore?

4. **Connect to the universal themes**
   - Match your observations to the universal themes that have been discussed in this chapter.

5. **Summarise the themes**
   - Write a one-sentence summary of the poem's main idea.

How themes shape poetry

Themes are the heart of a poem – they give the words purpose and meaning. Whether it's the universal experience of love or a deeply personal reflection on identity, themes help poets connect with their readers.

The way a poet explores a theme can vary widely. For example, love can be celebrated in one poem and mourned in another. Nature can be a source of peace or a force of destruction. As you read and write poetry, think about the themes that matter most to you and how you can express them through your words.

Poetry in practice – themes that matter

Your task

1. Reflect on the themes discussed in this chapter.
   - Which ones resonate most with you?
   - Are there any themes you think are missing?
2. Choose a theme and brainstorm specific ideas or images that relate to it.
   - This brainstorm can be in the form of a list, a mind map or sticky notes. Whatever helps get you thinking! For example, for the theme of nature, you might think of a favourite place, the sound of rain or a memory of being outdoors.

Portfolio connection

Save your brainstorm. It will serve as a starting point for more polished pieces in your portfolio.

Case study: Different takes on the same theme

Compare two poems that explore the same theme in different ways.

Theme: Love

1. **Romantic love:** Shakespeare's 'Sonnet 18'

   Shall I compare thee to a summer's day?
   Thou art more lovely and more temperate.

2. **Familial love:** Seamus Heaney's 'Follower'

   My father worked with a horse-plough,
   His shoulders globed like a full sail strung.

Discussion questions

1. How does each poet's approach to the theme shape the tone of their poem?
2. Which poem do you connect with more? Why?
3. Could you write a poem about the same theme but from your own perspective?

Final thought

Themes give poetry its power – they allow us to explore, express and connect. As you move forward, keep reflecting on the themes that matter most to you and how you can bring them to life in your writing.

Reflection

Revisit the three themes you wrote at the beginning of this chapter. Has your understanding of what poets write about changed? What new themes would you add to your list?

Activity: Theme exploration

Learning intention

To consolidate your understanding of themes in poetry by writing a thoughtful poem that reflects a theme you feel strongly about, while experimenting with structure and poetic devices.

Your task

Step 1: Choose your theme

Select a theme from this chapter (for example, love, nature, identity, loss or social and political issues) or a personal theme that resonates with you.

Step 2: Reflect on the theme

Write a short paragraph about why you chose this theme.

Consider questions like:

- Why does this matter to you?
- What emotions or memories does it bring up?

Step 3: Plan your poem

Decide on the form; will your poem follow a structure, like a sonnet? Or will you just go ham and write in free verse?

Brainstorm ideas or images related to your theme. For example:

- Love – a quiet moment shared with someone special.
- Nature – a memory of the ocean at sunset.
- Social issues – a time you witnessed or felt the need for change.

Step 4: Write your poem

Create a poem of 8–12 lines (or 14 if you're writing a sonnet) exploring your chosen theme.

Experiment with at least two poetic devices (for example, imagery, metaphor, sound).

Step 5: Reflect

Write a short reflection addressing the following questions:

- How did the theme influence your word choice and tone?
- Did you find it challenging to express your ideas? Why or why not?
- What did you learn about yourself or your writing through this activity?

Step 6: Portfolio connection

Save your poem and reflection for your portfolio. This entry will demonstrate your ability to engage deeply with a theme and use poetic devices to express your ideas.

CHAPTER 5

The art of word choice

Every word in a poem matters. Poets don't have the luxury of using too many words – they have to make every choice count. A single word can carry layers of meaning, evoke emotion or set the tone of a poem. It's not just about what the words mean, but how they sound, feel and interact with one another.

In this chapter, we'll explore how poets use word choice to create meaning. You'll learn to identify the impact of specific words, consider how language shapes tone and emotion, and experiment with using precise language in your own writing. By the end of the chapter, you'll understand how to read and write poetry with an eye for detail.

> **Before we begin**
>
> How do individual words shape the meaning of a poem? Write down three ways you think word choice matters. At the end of this chapter, you'll revisit your ideas to see if they've evolved.

How word choice shapes meaning

Poetry isn't about what's being said, it's about how it's being said. A poet's language choices can evoke emotions, create imagery and add layers of meaning. Here are some ways to unpack a poem's language:

Element	Definition	Example
Denotation	The literal meaning of a word (its dictionary definition)	*Home* means a place where someone lives
Connotation	The emotional, cultural or symbolic associations a word carries	*Home* connotes warmth, safety and family
Imagery	Language that appeals to the senses to create vivid mental pictures	*The golden sun sank low, sending fire into the sea* evokes a vivid image of a sunset
Symbolism	The use of objects, words or images that represent deeper meanings or ideas	In Judith Wright's *Train Journey*, 'the moon's cold sheet' symbolises detachment and loss
Sound and rhythm	The way words flow, repeat or emphasise meaning through sound pattern	The phrase 'confused hammering dark' in *Train Journey* mimics the rhythm of a train and reinforces the mood
Word choice	The poet's deliberate selection of words for their meaning, sound and emotional impact	In Langston Hughes' *Harlem*, 'dream deferred' evokes frustration and longing

Element	Definition	Example
Tone	The attitude or mood the poet conveys through their language	In Gwen Harwood's *In the Park*, the tone shifts from warmth to bitterness, reflecting the speaker's internal conflict
Patterns and echoes	The repetition of sounds, words or images to create unity or emphasis	In Oodgeroo Noonuccal's *We Are Going*, the repetition of 'we are' emphasises collective identity and cultural loss

Poetry in practice – say more with less

Your task

1. Choose an everyday object (for example, a cup of coffee, a book, a flower).
2. Write two descriptions of the object:
   - One using neutral or generic words
   - One using vivid, specific or sensory words (refer to the table above for help)

Reflect

How did your word choices change the tone or impact of your description?

Portfolio connection

Save your vivid description as part of your portfolio. It can serve as a foundation for a poem later.

Case study: Word choice in action

Poem excerpt: Oodgeroo Noonuccal's 'Municipal Gum'

> *Municipal gum, it is dolorous*
> *To see you thus,*
> *Set in your black grass of bitumen—*
> *O fellow citizen,*
> *What have they done to us?*

Annotations

1. **Imagery:** The juxtaposition of a gum tree and urban bitumen evokes a sense of displacement.

2. **Connotation:** Words like 'dolorous' and 'bitumen' emphasise unnaturalness and sorrow.

3. **Sound:** The soft alliteration of 's' in 'set in your black grass' contrasts with the harshness of 'b' in 'bitumen'.

Discussion questions

1. How does the image of the gum tree on 'black grass of bitumen' reflect the theme of displacement?

2. What feelings are evoked by the words 'dolorous' and 'bitumen'?

3. Why do you think the poet addresses the tree as a 'fellow citizen'?

Applying word choice in your own writing

Now that you've seen how poets like Oodgeroo Noonuccal carefully choose words to convey meaning, it's time to think about how you can do the same in your own writing. Here are some tips and tricks to think about:

Choose words with purpose

Think about the emotional or symbolic weight of each word. Words like 'bitumen' in 'Municipal Gum' carry not just a literal meaning but also a sense of displacement and harshness.

Experiment with imagery

Use descriptive language to create vivid mental pictures. Instead of saying, 'the sky was grey', try something like, 'A slate sky hung heavy, promising rain'. Think about how each sense – sight, sound, touch, taste and smell – can bring your poem to life.

Play with sound and rhythm

Choose words that complement the mood of your poem. Soft consonants (like *m, n* and *s*) can evoke calm, while harder sounds (like *t* and *k*) can create tension. Use repetition, alliteration and consonance to enhance the poem's tone.

Use contrast and juxtaposition

Pair unexpected or opposing words to create tension and interest. For example, 'the laughter echoed, sharp and hollow'.

Revise with intent

Poetry is about refining. Go back to a draft and look at each word critically. Ask yourself: does it contribute to the tone, mood or rhythm? Could another word do the job better?

Final thought

Every word in a poem matters. By choosing your words carefully, you can create powerful images, emotions and meanings that resonate with your readers.

> ### Reflection
>
> Revisit the three ways you wrote about word choice at the start of this chapter. How has your understanding of language and meaning evolved?

Activity: The perfect word

Learning intention

To consolidate your understanding of how word choice influences tone, meaning and emotion by writing a poem with precise and purposeful language.

Your task

Step 1: Choose a theme

Pick a theme that resonates with you. You can use a theme from earlier chapters or select a personal topic.

Step 2: Build your word bank

Brainstorm a list of words related to your theme. Focus on:

- **Connotation** – emotional associations of the words
- **Imagery** – sensory details that bring the theme to life
- **Sound** – words that enhance rhythm or mood

Step 3: Write your poem

Using your word bank, write a short poem (8–12 lines) that explores your theme. Focus on:

- Creating vivid images using precise words
- Enhancing tone through word choice and sound
- Conveying an emotion or ideas clearly

Step 4: Reflect

Write a brief paragraph answering these questions:

- How did you decide which words to include?
- Did any words feel especially powerful or surprising as you wrote?
- How did your word choices shape the tone or meaning of your poem?

Step 5: Portfolio connection

Save your poem and reflection for your portfolio as a demonstration of your ability to use language purposefully.

CHAPTER 6

Analysing poetry

Analysing a poem can feel overwhelming at first – where do you start, and how do you make sense of all the layers? The good news is that analysing poetry is like solving a puzzle; by breaking it down into manageable parts, you can uncover the meaning, emotions and artistry behind the words.

In this chapter, we'll use a simple framework – **What; How; Why; So** – to guide your analysis. This method will help you identify what's happening in a poem, how the poets use techniques to create meaning, why these choices matter and what the poem means overall. By the end of the chapter, you'll have the skills to confidently analyse any poem.

Before we begin

What steps do you take when trying to understand a poem? Write down your process in two to three sentences. At the end of the chapter, revisit your ideas to see how they align with this chapter's learning.

A framework: What; How; Why; So

Analysing poetry becomes easier with a clear approach. The **What; How; Why; So** framework breaks down the process into four simple steps. It helps you identify what's happening in the poem, how the poet creates meaning, why these choices are important and the larger ideas the poem conveys.

WHAT: What is happening in the poem?

This step focuses on identifying the subject and literal meaning of the poem.

Key questions

- What is the poem about?
- What images, events or ideas are presented?

HOW: How does the poet create meaning?

This step involves looking at the techniques the poet uses.

Key questions

- What poetic devices are used (for example, metaphor, imagery, rhyme)?
- How does the structure, rhythm or sound contribute to the meaning?
- Does the form indicate something about the poem's meaning?

WHY: Why are these techniques effective?

This step asks you to consider the purpose and impact of the poet's choices.

Key questions
- Why do these techniques matter?
- What emotions or ideas do they emphasise?

SO: So, what does it all mean?

This step ties everything together, focusing on the poem's overall meaning and themes.

Key questions
- What is the poet trying to say?
- How does the poem connect to larger themes or ideas?

Case study: Analysing Maya Angelou's 'Still I Rise'

Poem excerpt

You may write me down in history
With your bitter, twisted lies,
You may trod me in the very dirt
But still, like dust, I'll rise.

Using the framework

WHAT: What is happening in the poem?

The speaker addresses an oppressive force – likely societal injustice or personal prejudice – that seeks to diminish her. Despite this, the speaker declares her resilience and determination to rise above it, using dust as imagery to symbolise her strength and persistence.

HOW: How does the poet create meaning?

- **Imagery:** The comparison of rising 'like dust' evokes a sense of lightness, inevitability and natural resilience.
- **Repetition:** The phrase 'I'll rise' is repeated throughout the poem, reinforcing the speaker's unwavering confidence and defiance.
- **Tone:** The tone is both defiant and celebratory, conveying strength in the face of adversity.

WHY: Why are these techniques effective?

- The **imagery** of dust connects to universal themes of nature and resilience, making the speaker's triumph feel both personal and global.
- The **repetition** emphasises the speaker's confidence and resilience, turning the act of 'rising' into a rallying cry for others facing oppression.
- The **tone** invites the reader to feel empowered and inspired, transforming the speaker's personal struggle into a universal message.

SO: So, what does it all mean?

The poem is a declaration of resilience and empowerment, confronting systems of oppression and celebrating the indomitable human spirit. It inspires readers to persist in the face of adversity and find strength in their identity.

Discussion questions

1. How does the repetition of 'I'll rise' shape the tone and message of the poem?
2. What emotions does the image of rising 'like dust' evoke, and how does it connect to the theme of resilience?
3. How might this poem resonate differently with readers from various background or experiences?

Practising the framework

Now that you've seen how the **What; How; Why; So** framework can be applied to a poem, it's time to try it for yourself. Let's analyse an excerpt from Ocean Vuong's 'Someday I'll Love Ocean Vuong,' a deeply personal poem exploring identity, vulnerability and self-love.

> *The most beautiful part of your body*
> *Is where it's headed*
> *And remember,*
> *loneliness is still time spent*
> *With the world.*

Guided practice

Use the prompts to guide your analysis.

What

- What is happening in the poem?
- Example: The speaker reflects on their journey of self-acceptance, framing loneliness as a connection to the world.

How

- How does the poet create meaning?
- Example: Vuong uses abstract imagery (*the most beautiful part of your body is where it's headed*) to suggest growth and possibility, and a conversational tone to create intimacy with the reader.

Why

- Why are these techniques effective?
- Example: The abstract imagery invites readers to interpret the lines personally, while the tone encourages empathy and reflection on universal struggles with self-acceptance.

So

- So, what does it all mean?
- Example: The poem emphasises that self-love and acceptance are journeys, and even difficult emotions like loneliness can connect us to the larger human experience.

Your turn

Write your own analysis of Vuong's excerpt using the **What; How; Why; So** framework. Then, reflect on how this method helped you uncover the deeper layers of meaning in the poem.

Final thought

Analysing poetry is like uncovering a hidden message. With the **What; How; Why; So** framework, you now have the tools to decode any poem, finding meaning in its layers of language, sound and emotion. As you move forward, keep practising this skill to develop a deeper appreciation for the art of poetry.

Remember: Your interpretation is valid. Whatever comes to your mind when reading and then analysing a poem is CORRECT. The only thing you need to do is back up what you say. If you have the evidence from the text, then nobody can argue with you!

> ### Reflection
>
> Revisit the process you described at the start of this chapter. How does it compare with the **What; How; Why; So** approach? What steps will you add or change when analysing a poem in the future?

Activity: Your complete analysis

Learning intention

To consolidate your understanding of the framework by applying it to a full poem and creating a written analysis.

Your task

Step 1: Select a poem

Choose a poem from this chapter or the one you're studying in class.

Step 2: Use the framework

Write a paragraph for each step of **What; How; Why; So**:

- **What** is happening in the poem?
- **How** does the poet create meaning?
- **Why** are these techniques effective?
- **So**, what does it mean overall?

Step 3: Reflect

Write a short paragraph about your experience using the framework.

Did it help you understand the poem better?

Which step was the easiest or most challenging, and why?

Step 4: Portfolio connection

Save your completed analysis and reflection for your portfolio. This will demonstrate your ability to break down and interpret a poem using a structured approach, showing both critical thinking and engagement with the text.

CHAPTER 7

Writing about poetry

Analysing a poem is one thing – communicating your analysis effectively is another. Writing about poetry requires you to organise your thoughts clearly, provide evidence from the poem, and explain how and why the poet's choices create meaning. It's not just about summarising what happens in the poem but crafting an argument that digs into its deeper layers.

In this chapter, we'll build on the **What; How; Why; So** framework to structure your analytical writing. You'll learn how to develop a clear contention, use evidence to support your ideas and connect your analysis to larger themes. By the end of the chapter, you'll be able to write concise and insightful responses to poetry, whether for assignments, exams or your own reflections.

> ### Before we begin
>
> What do you think makes effective writing about poetry clear and effective? Write down three qualities of strong analytical writing. At the end of the chapter, revisit your list to see how it compares to the techniques you've learned.

The What; How; Why; So framework for writing

The **What; How; Why; So** framework isn't just for your analysis – it's also an approach for your analytical writing. Each paragraph you write about poetry should follow this structure:

What: Introduce the topic of your paragraph – what your paragraph will be focusing on.

- Clearly state the poem's focus or key ideas.
- Example: *Angelou's use of repetition emphasises the speaker's resilience and determination.*

How: Introduce evidence from the poem and explain the techniques the poet uses.

- Use specific examples from the poem to support your points.
- Example: *The recurring phrase 'I'll rise' creates a rhythmic affirmation of strength.*

Why: Analyse the effect of the poet's choices and why they're significant.

- Discuss how the poet's choices contribute to the meaning or emotion of the poem.
- Example: *This repetition reinforces the speaker's defiance and inspires readers to feel empowered.*

So: Conclude with a link to the broader significance or theme of the poem.

- Tie your analysis to larger themes or ideas, answering the question: Why does this poem matter?
- Example: *Through repetition, Angelou transforms personal resilience into a universal call for empowerment.*

Steps for writing an analytical response

1. Develop a clear contention

Your main contention is the main argument of your response. It should answer the question you're presented with, or the broader question: *What is the poet trying to achieve, and how?*

Example: Maya Angelou's 'Still I Rise' uses repetition, imagery and tone to assert her resilience and inspire others to overcome oppression.

2. Use evidence effectively

Every claim you make should be supported with evidence from the poem.

Tip: Embed short quotes into your sentences for smoother analysis. Don't just plonk a quote in!

Example: The metaphor of 'dust' in 'like dust, I'll rise' evokes persistence and inevitability, reinforcing the speaker's strength.

3. Explain your evidence

Don't just present quotes – analyse them. Explain why the evidence matters and how it supports your main contention.

Example: The repetition of 'I'll rise' creates a rhythmic, defiant tone, emphasising the speaker's unshakeable confidence.

4. Organise your writing

Follow a clear structure that mirrors the What; How; Why; So framework, like this:

Introduction: State your main contention and briefly introduce the poem.

Body paragraphs:

- Start with *What* and *How* (identify and explain techniques).
- Move to *Why* (analyse their impact).
- End with *So* (bringing your analysis back to the topic/the impact on the audience).

Conclusion: Restate your main contention, then explain how your paragraphs have answered the question. Leave your final sentence for something that will make your teacher/assessor think some profound thought that will blow their mind!

Case study: Writing about 'Still I Rise'

Question: How does Maya Angelou convey resilience in 'Still I Rise'?

Example paragraph

- **What:** In 'Still I Rise', Maya Angelou conveys resilience through repetition and imagery.
- **How:** The recurring phrase 'I'll rise' serves as both a declaration and a defiance, creating a rhythmic affirmation of strength. Angelou also uses the metaphor of 'dust' in 'like dust, I'll rise' to symbolise persistence and inevitability.
- **Why:** These techniques emphasise the speaker's unwavering confidence and inspires readers to find strength in their own struggles.
- **So:** Ultimately, the poem's defiant tone transforms personal resilience into a universal call for empowerment of marginalised communities.

Building blocks for analytical writing

Writing about poetry requires the right tools to clearly express yourself in your analysis. Using precise verbs and structured sentences helps you communicate your ideas effectively and with confidence.

This section provides you with practical language tools – common analytical verbs and sentence starters for the What; How; Why; So framework – to elevate your writing and ensure clarity.

Common analytical verbs	
Verb	**Example**
Conveys	The poet **conveys** a sense of nostalgia through vivid imagery
Emphasises	The repetition **emphasises** the speaker's determination
Explores	The poem **explores** the theme of loss through metaphor and tone
Reflects	The imagery **reflects** the speaker's inner conflict
Highlights	The contrast **highlights** the tension between freedom and control
Suggests	The metaphor **suggests** an underlying sense of hope
Reinforces	The rhyme **reinforces** the rhythmic, celebratory tone
Creates	The use of sound **creates** a sombre atmosphere
Symbolises	The broken clock **symbolises** the passage of time
Evokes	The language **evokes** a feeling of longing and melancholy
Portrays	The poet **portrays** the speaker as resilient and defiant
Develops	The shifting tone **develops** the poem's theme of transformation
Contrasts	The harsh consonants **contrast** with the poem's imagery
Challenges	The poem **challenges** traditional ideas of beauty and strength
Captures	The imagery **captures** the fleeting nature of happiness

	Sentence starters for What; How; Why; So
What	• The poem focuses on... • This stanza describes... • The speaker addresses... • The central theme of the poem is... • The imagery presents...
How	• The poet uses [technique] to... • Through [poetic device], the poet creates... • The repetition of [phrase] highlights... • The structure of the poem reflects... • The use of [symbol] conveys...
Why	• This technique is effective because... • The [device] emphasises the poem's theme of... • This creates a feeling of... • The metaphor suggests... • The poet's choice of [technique] adds depth by...
So	• Overall, the poem suggests... • This reflects the larger theme of... • The poem ultimately conveys... • Through these techniques, the poet highlights... • This analysis reveals the poem's exploration of...

Final thought

Writing about poetry isn't just about summarising a poem – it's about exploring its layers and communicating your understanding. By using the **What; How; Why; So** framework, you can craft well-structured paragraphs that bring your analysis to life.

> ### Reflection
>
> Revisit your ideas about what makes writing about poetry effective. How does the **What; How; Why; So** framework help you organise your thoughts and communicate them clearly?

Activity: Write your analysis

Learning intention

To consolidate your ability to write about poetry by crafting a series of structured analytical paragraphs.

Your task

Step 1: Select a poem

Choose a poem from this chapter, one you're studying in class or just one you're interested in.

Step 2: Plan your response

Break your analysis into multiple paragraphs, each focusing on a different technique or idea.

Step 3: Write your analysis

Use the **What; How; Why; So** framework for each paragraph:

- **Introduction** – state your main contention and the poem's focus.
- **Body paragraphs** – analyse specific techniques or themes in detail.
- **Conclusion** – summarise the poem's significance and connect it to broader ideas.

Step 4: Portfolio connection

Save your full analysis for your portfolio. This will demonstrate your ability to write clear, insightful paragraphs about poetry.

CHAPTER 8

Poetry through time and culture

When we read a poem written centuries ago, something magical happens. Despite the distance of time, despite changes in language and culture, we can still feel what that long-ago poet felt. We might recognise our own experiences in their words or understand emotions that haven't changed across centuries. This connection across time is one of poetry's most powerful features.

Poetry has existed as long as humans have had the desire to share their stories and feelings. It began around fires, in songs and chants, keeping alive the memories and wisdom of communities. As humans developed writing, poetry found new forms. Now, in our digital age, poetry continues to evolve, finding new ways to speak to new generations.

> ### Before we begin
> How do you think poetry has changed over time? What cultural influences do you think have shaped its development?

The evolution of poetry

The story of poetry is really the story of human communication. In the beginning, poetry lived in the human voice. It was the way people remembered their histories, celebrated their triumphs, mourned their losses and passed on their knowledge. The rhythm and patterns of poetry made it easier to remember long stories and important information.

Before writing, poets were keepers of memory. They memorised vast amounts of information – histories, laws, religious texts and cultural knowledge – all in the form of poetry. Some of these oral traditions, like First Nations songlines, continue today, showing us how ancient forms of poetry can remain vital and meaningful.

Universal themes through time

Ancient beginnings

| Stories passed down through generations | Songs carried news and history | Ceremonies marked important events | Poems helped people remember laws and teachings |

⬇

First Nations songlines

| Map Country | Share knowledge | Maintain culture | Connect people to place |

⬇

Classic to medieval

| New forms developed | Poets became professionals | Poetry spread between cultures | Rules and traditions formed |

⬇

The modern shift

| Free verse becomes popular | Personal experiences take centre stage | Everyday language enters poems | New forms emerge (concrete poetry, spoken word) |

Throughout history, poets have returned to the same fundamental human experiences: love, loss, nature, war, family and identity. What changes is not what poets write about, but how they express universal themes. By looking at how different eras handle the same subjects, we can see both what changes in poetry and what remains constant.

Think about how we tell stories today compared to how your grandparents might have told them. The core of the story might be the same, but the language, references and style would be different. Poetry works in the same way – the feelings and experiences remain recognisable even when the way of expressing them changes dramatically.

Love through time

Love has inspired poets for thousands of years, yet each era finds new ways to express this timeless emotion. The ancient Greek poet Sappho wrote of physical symptoms of love – trembling, speechlessness, burning sensations. Shakespeare used elaborate metaphors comparing lovers to nature. Modern poets often use more direct language, sometimes even incorporating text messages or social media references.

Here are three love poems from different periods:

Ancient (Sappho, 600 BCE)

Sweet mother, I cannot work the loom
I am broken with longing for a boy
by slender Aphrodite

Medieval (anonymous, 1200s)

Western wind, when wilt thou blow,
The small rain down can rain?
Christ, if my love were in my arms
And I in my bed again!

Modern (Warsan Shire, 2000s)

my love for you is stammering
i can't get the words out
right

War and conflict

How poets write about war has changed dramatically over time. Earlier war poetry often focused on glory and honour, while modern war poems tend to be more critical, focusing on the human cost and the futility of conflict.

Let's look at three poems from different periods:

1800s – Lord Tennyson's 'The Charge of the Light Brigade'

"Forward, the Light Brigade!
Charge for the guns!" he said.
Into the valley of Death
Rode the six hundred.

Here, even describing a military disaster, the poet emphasises bravery and noble sacrifice. The soldiers are presented as heroes, their death as glorious.

World War I – Wilfred Owen's 'Dulce et Decorum Est'

If you could hear, at every jolt, the blood
Come gargling from the froth-corrupted lungs,
Obscene as cancer, bitter as the cud
Of vile, incurable sores on innocent tongues...

By World War I, poets were showing war's brutal reality. Owen, who died in the war, wanted to show the truth behind phrases like 'it is sweet and fitting to die for one's country'.

Vietnam era – Bruce Dawe's 'Weapons Training'

And when I say eyes right I want to hear
those eyeballs click and the gentle pitter-patter
of falling dandruff you there what's the matter
why are you looking at me are you a queer?

Modern war poetry often uses irony and everyday language. Dawe's poem shows military training dehumanises both soldier and their trainers.

How war poetry changed

Early war poems often:
- Celebrated heroic deeds
- Used formal, elevated language
- Focused on glory and honour
- Encouraged patriotic feelings

Modern war poems tend to:
- Show war's psychological impact
- Use direct, sometimes brutal, language
- Question why we fight
- Focus on individual experiences

Today's war poets write about:
- The impact on families left behind
- The challenge of returning to civilian life
- The role of technology in modern warfare
- The effects of war on civilians
- The complexity of modern conflicts

Australia's poetry's story

The story of Australia's poetry is unique, weaving together one of the world's oldest continuous poetic traditions with more recent voices and forms. This rich mixture reflects our changing understanding of what it means to be Australian and what stories need to be told.

First Nations oral traditions

For tens of thousands of years, Aboriginal and Torres Strait Islander peoples have used poetry in its broadest sense – combining word, song, dance and art – to maintain culture and connection to Country. These poetic traditions are not historical artifacts, but living, breathing forms that continue to evolve and speak to contemporary audiences.

In these traditions, poetry is not separate from daily life. It is woven into:

- The sharing of knowledge about land
- The passing down of laws and customs
- The teaching of practical skills
- The celebration of significant events
- The maintenance of relationships between people and Country

Colonial voices (1788–1900)

When European settlers arrived in Australia, they brought their own poetic traditions. Soon, these forms began to adapt to the Australian experience. Poets found themselves trying to describe landscapes and experiences that didn't fit neatly into European poetic conventions.

The bush ballad emerged as one of the first distinctly Australian poetic forms. Poets like Banjo Paterson and Henry Lawson developed a style that:

- Used everyday language
- Told stories of rural life
- Celebrated (and sometimes criticised) the bush myth
- Created enduring cultural images

Modern Australian poetry

Contemporary Australian poetry reflects our multicultural, predominantly urban society. Modern Australian poets write about:

- City and suburban life
- Environmental concerns
- Cultural identity
- Indigenous perspectives
- Migration experiences
- Personal relationships
- Political issues

Poets like Oodgeroo Noonuccal, Judith Wright, Les Murray, Sarah Holland-Batt and Ali Cobby Eckermann have helped create a poetry that speaks to and about modern Australia while acknowledging its complex history.

Final thought

Poetry is a living art form, shaped by the people and cultures that create it. By exploring its journey through time and across culture, you've gained a deeper appreciation for how poetry reflects humanity's shared experiences and endless creativity.

> ### Reflection
>
> Revisit your thoughts from the start of this chapter. How has your understanding of poetry's evolution and cultural diversity changed? What new insights or inspirations have you gained?

Activity: Cultural connections in poetry

Learning intention

To understand how cultural and historical contexts shape poetry by analysing and reflecting on a specific poetic tradition.

Your task

Step 1: Select a poem

Choose a poem from this chapter, or another one that represents a specific cultural tradition.

Step 2: Analyse it

Use the **What; How; Why; So** framework to unpack a poem's historical and social context:

- **What** is the poem about?
- **How** does it reflect its cultural or historical context?
- **Why** is this context significant to its meaning?
- **So**, what can we learn about the culture or era from this poem?

Step 3: Reflect

Write a short paragraph about how this poem connects to broader cultural or historical themes discussed in this chapter.

Step 4: Portfolio connection

Save your analysis and reflection to demonstrate your ability to connect poetry to its cultural and historical roots.

CHAPTER 9

Poetry in the digital age

Think poetry only lives in dusty books and the English classroom? Think again! Poetry isn't just changing – it's exploding into new forms and spaces. This chapter explores how poetry lives and breathes into today's world, and how you can be a part of it.

In this chapter, we'll explore how technology is shaping the world of poetry. From Instagram poets and the spoken word on YouTube to AI-generated and multimedia projects, you'll see how digital tools are redefining what poetry can be. By the end, you'll reflect on how you might use these tools to share your own poetic voice.

> **Before we begin**
>
> How do you think technology has changed the way we create, share and experience poetry?

New forms of poetry

Traditional poetry lived on the printed page. Today's poetry might be:

Platform	Features	Examples
Instagram	Visual and text	Short poems with images
TikTok (assuming it's not banned)	Performance and music	60-second spoken word
Twitter/X	Micro poetry	Haiku, short verses
Digital games	Interactive text	Choose-your-path poems
Apps	Collaborative writing	Group poetry projects

Digital poetry in action

Traditional poems stay the same each time you read them. Digital poetry can be dynamic, interactive and different with each reading. Poetry has found new life online through:

- **Hypertext poems** – clickable paths let readers explore the poem in unique ways.
- **Interactive verses** – reader choices shape the poem.
- **Multimedia poems** – combines words, sounds and visuals to create layered experiences.
- **Generative poetry** – crafted with AI or coding, these poems evolve based on inputs.

Here's how a hypertext poem might look like:

> Click here
> > to discover
> > > more words
> > > > creating paths
> > > > > through language

(There are no links in this example, but you get the idea!)

From screen to experience

Digital poetry isn't just words on a screen – it's an experience that changes with each interaction. Some poems only exist in digital space because they:

- Respond to reader clicks
- Change based on time of day
- Generate new combinations
- Include sound and movement
- React to reader choices

Think of it like the difference between reading about a video game and playing one. These poems need technology to come alive. Popular platforms and apps include:

Poetry apps	What they do
Poet's Pad	Helps generate ideas and rhymes
Poem Generator	Builds different forms, based on themes and key words
Synthetic Poetry	Collaborates with AI to write poetry
Word Mover	Creates magnetic poetry digitally

Explore these tools – or discover your own – to bring poetry into the digital age.

Making digital poetry

Want to create your own digital poetry? Here are some starting points for you:

Basic tools	Advanced creation
Start with: • Notes app on your phone • Simple recording device • Basic photo editor • Social media account • Digital art app	Move up to: • Website builders • Animation software • Sound-mixing tools • Video editors • Coding platforms

Poetry and performance

Think of slam poetry as the difference between reading about a song and hearing it live. When poets perform their work, they use:

Body language	Voice	Space
Gestures	Volume	Stage movement
Facial expressions	Pace	Audience interaction
Posture	Tone	Energy flow
Movement	Silence	Direction

Modern performance poets have transformed poetry from a quiet, solitary experience into a dynamic, shared event. They've brought poetry out of books and onto stages, street corners and social media platforms.

Getting started with slam

Before you perform your first slam poem:

1. Write for the ear, not the eye.
2. Practise your timing.
3. Use repetition for impact.
4. Build to a strong ending.
5. Connect with your audience.

Performance styles

Different poetry performances require different approaches:

Slam poetry	Spoken word	Open mic
• Competitive format • Time limits (usually 3 minutes) • No props or music • Scored by judges • High-energy delivery	• More relaxed format • Can use music/props • Flexible length • Focus on storytelling • Personal style important	• Casual atmosphere • Mixed styles welcome • Supportive environment • Great for practice • Community focused

Poetry installations

Poetry isn't confined to pages – as we have learned. Poetry can also transform physical spaces into immersive experiences. A poetry installation turns words into an environment you can walk through, interact with or discover unexpectedly.

Types of installations

Format	Description	Example
Wall poetry	Text on building walls	Poems painted on school corridors
Path poetry	Sequential discoveries	Words embedded in garden paths
Window poetry	Light and transparency	Poems on glass that change with light
Interactive displays	Touch-activated text	Digital screens with moving poems
Hidden poetry	Surprise locations	QR codes linking to poems

Creating an installation

Think of a poetry installation like directing a movie – you're not just sharing words; you're creating an experience. Every choice you make, from the location to the font size, impacts how people discover and interact with the poetry. When designing your poetry installation, consider these elements:

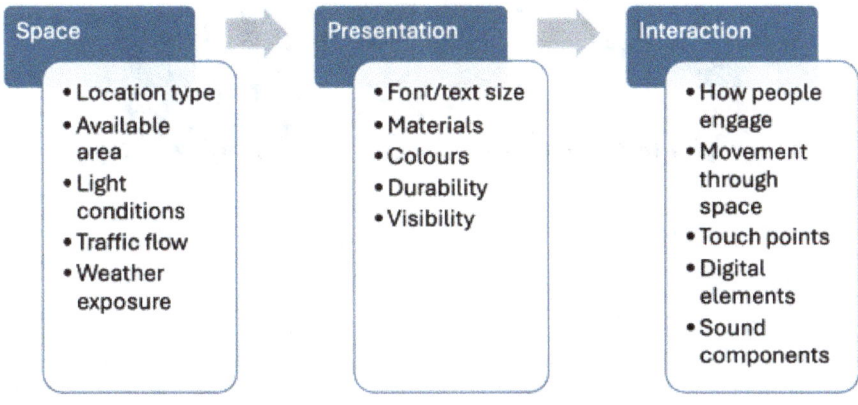

Space
- Location type
- Available area
- Light conditions
- Traffic flow
- Weather exposure

Presentation
- Font/text size
- Materials
- Colours
- Durability
- Visibility

Interaction
- How people engage
- Movement through space
- Touch points
- Digital elements
- Sound components

Poetry in the digital age

Final thought

The digital age is redefining what poetry can be. By embracing new tools and platforms, poets are reaching wider audiences, experimenting with form and pushing the boundaries of creative expression. As you explore the possibilities of digital poetry, remember that your voice is part of this exciting revolution.

> ### Reflection
>
> Revisit your thoughts from the start of this chapter. How has your understanding of poetry's place in the digital world evolved? What excites you most about the possibilities of digital poetry?

Activity: Create your poetry project

Learning intention

To explore, create and present poetry in innovative ways by engaging with digital tools, performance or interactive formats.

Your task

Step 1: Choose your path

Select ONE of the following poetry projects to develop and present:

Digital poetry collection	Performance piece	Poetry installation
Develop a multimedia poem that includes: • Written text • Visual elements • Interactive features • Sound/movement Platform options: Instagram story, website or digital presentation (PowerPoint, Canva, Keynote)	Develop a spoken word piece: • Write for performance • Add movement/gesture notes • Record a practice version • Get feedback • Polish final draft	Design a poetry display for a space: • Choose your location • Plan the layout • Include interactive elements • Consider your audience • Add multimedia aspects

Step 2: Develop your idea

Whatever path you choose, follow these steps to success:

Planning	Creation	Reflection
• Brainstorm your concept • List required elements • Note practical needs • Consider your audience	• Develop your piece, incorporating the required elements • Experiment with different approaches to find what works best • Revise and adjust based on feedback and testing • Polish the final details to ensure your project is cohesive and impactful	Write a short paragraph addressing these prompts: • Why did you choose this format? • What challenges did you face during the process? • How did this format influence the way you wrote or presented your poetry? • What would you do differently if you were to repeat the project?

Step 3: Portfolio connection

Save your completed project and reflection for your portfolio as a demonstration of your ability to innovate and adapt poetry to modern forms and contexts.

CHAPTER 10

Your poetry portfolio

This final chapter helps you bring together everything you've learned about poetry – reading it, writing it, analysing it and sharing it. Your portfolio will showcase your journey with poetry and your growing skills as both reader and writer.

What makes a strong portfolio?

Think of your portfolio as telling the story of your relationship with poetry. It should show:

- Your understanding of poetry
- Your development as a writer
- Your analytical skills
- Your creative process
- Your personal voice

Portfolio elements

Essential components	Purpose	Examples
Poetry analysis	Shows understanding	Written responses to poems
Original poetry	Demonstrates creativity	Your own poems in different styles
Reflections	Reveals thinking	Notes on your writing process
Experiments	Shows development	Attempts at different forms
Influences	Shows awareness	Poems that inspired you

Building your collection

1. **Poetry analysis (your reader's journey)**
   - Analyse multiple poems, comparing themes, techniques and styles.
   - Include personal responses and critical reflections.

2. Original poetry collection (your creative journey)

Style	Purpose	Include
Free verse	Personal expression	Two to three poems showing different approaches to poetry
Traditional forms	Technical skill	At least one sonnet, haiku or ballad
Performance	Vocal expression	Include spoken work scripts and links to video/audio recordings
Response poems	Literary engagement	Write poems inspired by other works with brief explanations

3. Process and development

Your poetry journey is about more than just final pieces. Showing your process demonstrates how you think, learn and develop as a writer – something teachers LOVE to read. Keep track of:

Stage	What to include	Why it matters
Inspirations	Sources, triggers, ideas	Shows what moves you to write
Planning	Mind maps, word lists, notes	Reveals your thinking process
Drafting	All versions, changes made	Demonstrates development
Feedback	Comments from others, workshops	Shows openness to growth
Revision	What changed and why	Reveals decision-making
Final	Finished piece plus reflection	Completes the journey

Organising your portfolio

Your portfolio tells a story – how you organise it shapes how others experience your poetry journey. Here are three ways to arrange your work:

Chronological	Thematic	Style-based
• Shows development over time • Highlights improvement • Reveals turning points	• Groups similar topics • Shows different approaches • Creates connections	• Separates different forms • Highlights technical range • Shows experimentation

Presenting your portfolio

Your portfolio deserves a professional presentation that shows the care you've put into your work. Consider these format options that best showcase your poetry journey:

Digital collection

Using PowerPoint, Canva, Keynote or Google Slides:

- Create a clear contents page.
- Display one poem per slide.
- Include drafts and notes.
- Add images thoughtfully.
- Use consistent fonts/colours.

Here's an example layout you may like to follow:

1. Contents
2. About me/introduction
3. Section 1: Poetry analysis
   a. Analysis 1 plus reflection
   b. Analysis 2 plus reflection
4. Section 2: My poetry
   a. Poem 1 plus drafts
   b. Poem 2 plus drafts
5. Reflections/growth

Physical portfolio

Using a display folder:

- Have clear section dividers.
- Include plastic sleeves for protection.
- Add labels and headings.
- Leave space for drafts.
- Save room for notes.

Here's a guide to organising your physical portfolio:

Section	Contents	Presentation
Opening	Title page, contents	Clean, professional
Analysis	Response to poems	Clear headings
Creative	Your poetry	Original work plus drafts
Process	Notes plus drafts	Show development
Reflection	Growth and goals	Thoughtful connection

Websites

Using free platforms, structure your poetry website like this:

- Create a homepage with an introduction.
- Use separate pages for different poetry types.
- Display blog-style reflection posts.
- Save space for multimedia elements.
- Include links between related pieces.

Key terms

This section explains important terms and concepts introduced throughout the book. Use it as a reference to clarify your understanding as you explore poetry.

Poetic devices	
Alliteration	The repetition of the same consonant sounds at the beginning of closely connected words (for example, *Peter Piper picked a peck of pickled peppers*).
Allusion	A reference to a person, place, event or work of literature, often implying deeper meaning.
Assonance	The repetition of vowel sounds in nearby words (for example, *The rain in Spain falls mainly on the plain*).
Caesura	A deliberate pause or break in a line of poetry, often marked by punctuation.
Consonance	The repetition of consonant sounds at the beginning of words (for example, *She sells seashells*).
Enjambment	When a sentence or phrase runs over from one line of poetry to the next without a pause.
Hyperbole	Exaggeration for effect (for example, *I've told you a million times*).
Imagery	Descriptive language that appeals to the senses (for example, *The golden sun spilled across the horizon*).

Irony	A contrast between expectation and reality, often used for humour or emphasis.
Juxtaposition	Placing two contrasting ideas, images or words close together for effect.
Metaphor	A direct comparison between two unlike things (for example, *Hope is a thing with feathers*).
Personification	Giving human qualities to non-human things (for example, *The wind whispered through the trees*).
Simile	A comparison using 'like' or 'as' (for example, *Her smile was like sunshine*).
Symbolism	Using an object or action to represent a deeper meaning (for example, *A dove representing peace*).

Poetic forms

Ballad	A narrative poem, often set to music, with a consistent rhyme scheme and rhythm.
Blackout poetry	A type of found poetry created by blacking out words in a text to leave a poem behind.
Elegy	A poem reflecting on loss or mourning.
Free verse	Poetry that does not follow regular patterns of rhyme or rhythm.
Haiku	A traditional Japanese form with three lines (5-7-5 syllables) often focusing on nature.
Limerick	A humorous poem with five lines and a specific rhyme scheme (AABBA).
Ode	A poem that celebrates or praises a person, event or object.

Slam poetry	Performance-based poetry that emphasises rhythm, voice and emotion.
Sonnet	A 14-line poem, often written in iambic pentameter, with a specific rhyme scheme.

Analysis terms	
Connotation	The emotional or cultural associations of a word, beyond its literal meaning.
Denotation	The literal, dictionary definition of a word.
Mood	The atmosphere or emotional setting created by the poem.
Perspective	The point of view or stance of the speaker in the poem.
Speaker	The narrative voice in the poem, not to be confused with the poet. The speaker may represent a character, perspective or abstract voice.
Theme	The central idea or message explored in a poem.
Tone	The attitude or mood conveyed by the poet's language.

	Structure and sound elements
Iambic pentameter	A common meter with five pairs of unstressed and stressed syllables per line.
Meter	The rhythmic structure of a poem, determined by the arrangement of stressed and unstressed syllables.
Rhyme scheme	The pattern of rhymes at the end of lines in a poem (for example, ABAB).
Stanza	A grouped set of lines within a poem, often separated by a blank line.
Volta	A shift or turning point in a poem, often found in sonnets.

www.ingramcontent.com/pod-product-compliance
Lightning Source LLC
Chambersburg PA
CBHW052109070526
44584CB00017B/2397